Something Completely Weird

poems, proverbs and stuff

by Chris Dyer

Monday Creek Publishing
Ohio USA

poems, proverbs, and stuff

Copyright © Chris Dyer 2017

Printed in the United States of America

Monday Creek Publishing, Ohio, USA
mondaycreekpublishing.com

From the Author

*A*s a writer (and many other things as well!) I use my limited imagination to weave my tales. I enjoy writing as I am now as the rain pounds, the ground outside and my dog sits beside me, head on my lap wondering why I am tapping away at these strange buttons rather than stroking his rather handsome head.

It makes you think a little deeper, animals have such remarkable honesty, my horses are the same, each treats me with devotion even if I am stamping around blaming the world for my mistakes. Now what if we started to care about each other and this beautiful planet we are privileged to call our home? Imagine if everybody gave one penny every day to a worthy cause, that would equal, assuming 40 million people in a position to do so in this country, and remember it is just one penny. It doesn't sound a lot does it, one penny, but that equals about £2,800,000 a week! Which is around £109,600,000 a year! Now imagine if ALL the wealthier countries did the same… How much would that be… then imagine that the governments gave a little back… idealistic I know, but not beyond the realms of possibility, let's say a penny of every £100 tax collected. How long would it take us to stamp out poverty, hunger, abuse? In doing so it might even bring us all a little closer, so maybe there would be less war

I'm not talking about just humans, let's be honest we are one of the later animals to place our feet upon this Earth, I'm talking about helping everything, humans, the other animals that dwell upon this earth with us and the earth itself. I'm no hippy, I'm not a vegetarian, and before you all start thinking I'm some sort of religious nut, I have belief but I'm not a religious fanatic. I do think we have a duty to stand together and protect that which we are guardians of! Don't forget our children inherit our mismanagement! So the next time you're stood fiddling in your pocket or purse perhaps you would give this some thought.

Oh, and one more thing, would all the fanatics and those with religious piety answer me a question or two. Why, when you are all saying the same about God wanting mankind to be just and kind to each other, are we kicking the shit out of each other? What makes you all so sure that you have the right religion and so don't those with different views have the right to those views, or do you just believe in dictatorship? One more! Can't stop when I start! Who wrote all your bibles regardless of your personal religious title for the book? The last one I can answer for you. It was man, the same as you and I, with the same faults, the same prejudices and probably just as opinionated as me! I wonder what your God would make of it? There is no excuse for us, and all the people that rant and rave, telling others they are wrong and trying to enforce it with violence, hurting women, children and those that have never raised a hand against them... what have you achieved? You are despised by all, even the people you call your own, you are not even honest. You do not create such atrocities for a greater good, you do it for your own warped self-belief, your own gratification. You are the sinners and I hope that whatever Heaven you think you go to your punishment will fit your greed. There can be no forgiveness for you, I am sure. Colour, creed or religion - we are or rather should be one people, one Earth, one... together!

When you've considered that think of this. Listen to a playground full of children anywhere in the world, listen very carefully... they all sound the same. Just remember the penny!

ONE BRIGHT BIRD

One bright bird that stands alone,

Surrounded by such darkness,

One bright bird that takes from all the grey,

All around lives yet in decay creeping oozing,

One bright bird, a rising sun,

Closing trying to devour, the light drives it back,

One bright bird stands out still.

NOW

Shake the hand of the man you do not know,

Kiss the cheek you have never seen before,

Smile as you walk by and nod your head,

Do not run from the scream, offer help,

Turn to instead of turn away from another,

Try to be calm in a tense situation,

Hold up your hands when another clenches theirs,

Judge yourself before you judge another,

Offer forgiveness before anger,

Use wisdom before stupidity,

Now you are a man.

LOST

Cars flash by,

No time, not really going anywhere just flashing by,

Lights blaze burning eyes,

Not really lighting anything,

Rivers run,

Not taking note of the surroundings,

Children laugh and cry,

The sound is lost to humanity.

WEDDING

I can now talk to it!

I sit with it on my lap,

No need to press the keys,

It answers me!!!!

Send an email and it goes.

Type a letter and it does,

Perhaps if I tell it to go to the bathroom it will?!

I now name this Dell your lawfully wedded laptop!

FOOLS PARADISE

How do we control emotion?
It runs riot through our veins,
No pill to take no vaccine,
Just, the never-ending ache,
We fool ourselves and the fool jumps in,
No doctors cure,
Stupidity is our own doing,
No reality here dreams take over,
But we wake from dreams,
Then face the light of day,
But always night returns to dream,
Cost that cannot be counted,
Fear that cannot be faced,
So, crawl into your cocoon,
Will the butterfly emerge,
Eaten by a passing sparrow,
The husk left dry and empty,
Another fool another heart,
But one day the fools may rise,
One day the wheel will turn,
What then when opportunity has passed you by,
What then will you fool,
Only yourself and the pain that will come.

TRY

Upon my skin I feel the pain,

Within my mind I see,

My heart tells me different and I listen,

My head tells me no!

I know it is inevitable,

I know the pain will be no less,

Yet still I try.

An endless circle that has no end.

I search to find respite,

But it eludes me and I know it will.

Yet still I try,

I withstand the pain,

It sears my soul,

Tears my heart,

It is all for nothing,

No more than a few empty words,

More lies without seeming reason,

Yet still I try.

CAN I?

Can I laugh at myself when all is lost?

Can I relieve my own pain?

Can I stop my own stupidity?

Can I stop the pain that I feel?

Can I change who I am?

Can I decide not to care?

Can I be someone else?

Can I wish that I was?

Life will not stop and sadly neither will I.

THE COMMODITY

A world of scorn as videos play,

Art? Or candy?

We watch fascinated when we should listen,

When all is quiet and still,

No more rhythmic beat,

No more lights what then?

No pleasure will you gain,

As they sit and watch the tiny screen,

Their comments raw,

As they nudge a friend, suggest and make lewd gestures,

Cans crushed and empty on the floor,

Laughter in the belief it was for them,

Straining closer to the screen in hope,

And you?

Sit alone in a bare apartment,

Are you used, are you fooled?

As much as I, I think.

FORGOTTEN

What would you wish if given a choice?

What would you choose for yourself?

It is one wish and one wish only and must be for you,

You cannot change the world,

You cannot help mankind,

It is just one choice and for you,

Would it be immortality per

haps?

Or looks as fair as any?

To have untold wealth?

Or for all the pain you suffer to be forgotten?

FIVE LEAVES MORE

I once led beneath her,

Her five leaves left,

Near naked but still beautiful,

Slender, elegant, inspiring,

Her shade cooling,

Her rebirth is beginning,

Soon she will again be dressed in green,

Dazzling as sunrays touch her,

As beautiful but so different,

She stands now dressed in green.

HOPE

In every dawn there comes new hope,

There must be,

The dream you had fades as the day begins,

Perhaps passion or sorrow, perhaps love or money,

Today will be better,

Today your dream will come true,

Or maybe tomorrow,

There is always hope.

A POEM

I read a poem,

It moved me,

What was it, it was mixed,

Of passion, sadness, loathing,

Something given and something lost,

Yet something to be renewed,

Despair and anger,

Yet fondness,

I was moved,

I saw you lying there aware,

Eyes blinking yet eyes open,

I was moved.

INVULNERABLE FOOL

How we fool ourselves,
Parents object yet we do not listen,
We believe we are invulnerable,
What shall we do when time goes by?
What shall we do when they see?
Can we deny it for there it is?
Recorded for eternity,
We think we are invulnerable,
It may not be suitable for some viewers,
A warning before you play,
It was not for me I have to say,
Now a cozy requirement that will not come,
We believe we are invulnerable,
An offer that has been made,
Now made to you, will you accept?
I think not the shadow is too great,
We think we are invulnerable,
Where will you go?
What next, another step?
Another video not on the stage?
We think we are invulnerable?
An offer of a hand,
An offer of change,
Laughed at, disparaged,
We think we are invulnerable,
To be a joke among friends,
For what honesty?
How we fool ourselves.

THE AGENCY

It is a game it's played with keys,
With someone that one never sees,
They watch the screen to read what's there,
Yet all it is, is pure hot air,
What lies behind it you may ask,
That bring so many to the task,
The promise of a life so fair,
Of beauty, love and care,
I did research so I could tell,
If there was one that did so well.
But in the main it was not true,
Money is the key to you,
You work and sweat, run back home,
Or when at work you use your phone,
Every time the credits leave,
Another message write me please,
But when the night is dark and cold,
You'll find that all you've been is sold,
There is no rainbow, there is no dream,
And all for something never seen.
Just one more thing before I go,
All their friends will laugh you know,
And all that they will beg and plead,
Another message write me PLEASE,
The credit card is looking bare,
But make no bones they do not care,
So here is a poem made for you,
It is a lie it is not true.

HOW?

How beautiful you are,

As precious as a diamond,

As innocent as new fell snow,

As kind as a mother,

How can you be so wonderful?

And yet your beauty holds a deadly venom.

Worse than any snake,

For a snake's bite gives pain but can be cured,

You know your bite will last forever,

What gain is there?

What advantage?

Is it because you know you can?

The power corrupts you?

You mesmerise but I do not think it is enough,

I think you need the fix,

To know that all are in awe with you.

One day though the dripping fangs will break,

And the very tears you cause will burn upon your own

cheeks.

JESTER

Laugh at me for I am the Jester,

Brought to court for merriment sake,

You only see the bright colours and bells,

The tumbles and foolishness,

I bring you laughter as I fall,

More, more, you cry,

For you lift my sadness,

Who is there for me?

Who will lift my sorrows?

Who will make me laugh,

Laugh at me for am I not the Jester.

INKY

Ink, ink what am I?

I have eight arms and rather shy?

I hide by day and out at night,

I do not hurt but I can bite,

Sometimes I am hard to see,

Because just like a rock I'll be,

I jet around so quietly,

Tell me now what could I be?

LIVING ART

An art gallery I stroll to see,

Yet miss the art that circles me,

Look there the Mona Lisa walks,

Should I approach, make small talk?

Then from the corner of my eye,

Another artwork I espy,

I would comment if it was paint,

But as its real I have restraint,

So politically correct have we become,

We lose our voice we are humdrum,

Now I don't care what I should say,

You do look beautiful today,

I look around and all is art,

From my lips the words I part,

Politically I do not care.

And do it without turn of hair.

ONE SMALL THING

Reach out your hand, it will cost you naught,

Speak one word the coin stays in your pocket,

Yet you give more with those simple gestures than

gold,

You give hope, you give pleasure,

A spring in the others step, a feeling of wellbeing,

And how much better do you feel?

See how you walk straighter,

One good thing for them is a far greater thing for you.

NO MORE

No more sabre rattling, no more blood,

No suffering of children,

We will not stand it,

It has no reason other than greed,

For your own selfish aims of power,

You puff out your chest and talk a fight,

But it is the innocent that suffer as you cower in the corner out of sight,

It is not your sons and daughters that are lost,

It is not you that sees the horrors, the gore,

You sit with your glass of wine a steak upon your plate,

It is not for you to cause such horrors to others,

Your standing has no right to this,

You are not there to kill and maim,

You are there to better all,

Not just your own pathetic ego,

No more sabre rattling, no more blood.

WHAT?

What do I see? What do I hear?

Shouted in anger the fall of a tear,

The one look of anguish, the sorrow, the pain,

Yet all could be saved if you just show restrain,

Much better to smile, to hug and to kiss,

Then all, of the sorrow is sure to be missed.

ROUND

I am so round that you can't see,

The beginning or the end of me,

I float in air yet hold you firm,

And yet you rape and slash and burn.

Without me you cannot keep life,

Yet all the time you bring me strife,

I let you stay and give my all,

Upon my skin I let you crawl,

My bounty given you still want more,

One day I'll pay you back for sure,

I bring you all it is you need,

And in return you just show greed.

Who am I, and what are you?

INK INK

Today a man drew on my arm,

With needles and artistic charm,

A tattooed man I have to say,

Artwork till my dying day,

Because I have a little ink,

It does not mean I do not think,

I am no different than before,

So judge me not I do implore.

HAPPY?

I am a happy person,

Yet still I sit alone,

No comfort just me,

Some think that I am clever,

A few think I am mad,

Even one or two that think that I am bad.

Still I am a happy person,

I breathe and live each day,

I smile and laugh I do not cry,

I do get angry, I am quite bold,

I have such love to give,

Yet still I am alone.

I LIVE IN A HOUSE

I live in a house yet we are friends,

We drive each other round the bend,

We laugh and joke and laugh some more,

We are good friends of that I'm sure,

If one is down and feeling blue,

They try their best to cheer up you,

We never judge, but tell the truth,

We all live beneath one roof.

THINK

When the bottle is tipped,

And nothing is left,

Do you now feel much better?

Look at the bottom,

The glass is now clear,

Your head may be spinning,

But nothing has changed,

Problems confronted are never solved,

At the base of a bottle or hiding the truth,

In the morning it hits you,

Like a runaway train,

No peace for the wicked,

No escape from the pain,

So, take heed my friend,

And listen to me,

We all must face life,

We are what we are,

Me I am stupid,

And yet I'm no fool,

I am nowhere near perfect,

I hope for a dream that never will come.

DANCE

Is it a dance that I see?
Or music played?
Watched, desired?
For the music or for the sight?
The promise of something more…. Hope?
Power, control, possession of the audience?
Will the flames scorch and sear the flesh?
Lights blinding, is it real?
It is an illusion, you watch entranced,
Another night of naked dance.
But whose tears fall when all is still?
Yours, I think not?
Maybe the dancer?
You will watch again,
Pathetic as you leer at what you see?
Perhaps even bragging more than your tiny screen
displays?
Commodities to be commercialised?
What have we become that we convince them it is
only art?
What will their future be when others see?
What will the husband or children think?
Their wife their mother……?
Even I could shed a tear in regret.

GUS 2

Hers's a little story,

It's about a little dog,

His head is on my feet and he's looking at me odd,

I scratch his ears and that's okay,

I'm sure he's trying hard to say,

Come on, you're boring we should play,

For his ball I look around,

And sure enough, he starts to bound,

He drives me nuts I have to say,

He does this to me everyday,

Would I change it? No Sirree,

Though wish I had his energy,

He never stops or judges me,

He is our Gus and sets us free.

STICKY

I am quite sticky to the touch,

Most do not like me very much,

I cannot run and get away,

I only travel yards a day,

I work by night it is my way,

Inside my house I often stay,

I am not lady or a man,

Can you work out what I am?

WHY

We do not see ourselves,

Oh, we look into the mirror but do not see,

We look back on time with pride,

Look we can fly to the moon,

We are supreme, we are the best,

History will tell a different story,

We will not admit but the truth cannot lie,

See what we have done,

Where man goes, death follows,

Not satisfied with the death of others we turn
upon ourselves,

What reason do we have?

If we are so great surely there is another way?

Harmony seems beyond our reach,

So are we clever?

Not as clever as we think,

So much progress yet so much we miss,

Why?

A dog may have sharp teeth but can still give comfort.

Is an empty plate better than no plate at all?

A horse is graceful but has a vicious kick.

A lie is like a match, to keep the fire burning you must get another from the box.

We are all children but need to grow up.

When God made man... she was only kidding!

When you pray remember more than yourself.

Who is the bigger fool? The man that shouts? Or the one that shouts back?

There is only one thing to fear... fear itself.

A mirror will show you who you are but not what you are.

If I had one brain cell less you would have to water me.

Hell is not living, it is not living.

Heaven is when you reach out a helping hand.

A PEG

I am a square peg,

They try to force me into a round hole,

A horse in a herd of cows,

Neither laughed at not taken seriously,

Scornful of bureaucrats,

Principled, morals lived by,

Honest even though it pains,

A tree in the middle of an ocean,

Uncaring of your disdain,

Moved by emotion,

Lost and yet found,

Loving yet angry,

Caring and yet cold,

I am me I can be no one else,

I shall remain a square peg in a round hole.

What will you be?

Will you fly with me?

STILL LOOKING

My feet begin to itch again,

I have to find my place,

To travel and to journey,

To seek respite and lay my head,

If only I could settle knowing one was there,

To hold a hand and be at one,

To wake and smile,

To sip on morning light,

This time I think I might!

WHAT A DRAG

You turn me slowly in your hand,

You press your fingers into me,

Light a fire sucking the very body from me,

Hot inflamed, you press me to your lips,

How you treat me,

Tossing me away when through.

What am I?

RED, RED...

A glass of wine is what I need,

The juice of grape without the seed,

The wondrous feeling... not too much,

As glasses clink and fingers touch,

A sip, a smile and to the floor,

Embraced in dance forever more,

A glass of wine is what I need,

But not too much you must take heed,

The memories that you then take,

Upon your face a smile will make.

EXTINCT

What did we do from spear and arrow?
To steel and lead so more of us can wind up
dead,
Split the atom make it bad our scientists are
going mad,
Let's melt the icecaps just for fun, now learn to
paddle not to run.
Ooh! We nearly missed let's burn the forest,
smoke not mist,
What is that species not one of us we'll run it
over with a bus,
Hang on. there in water something left pour in
rubbish till its bereft,
Now that we have cleared the seas, there
nothing left but us… your pleased?
Hang on what will we eat? Now that everything's
deplete.
You've brought the Earth down to its knees there
is no air you killed the trees,
Now your children stand and stare, at nothing for
there's nothing there,
A moment more before you think, it's now man's
turn to be extinct!

TIME

We pass by many as we go,

Wrapped up in ourselves,

Not caring not thinking too busy,

We have the largest brain yet do not think,

There is no time yet even time is manmade,

The watch upon your wrist, the screen upon your
mobile,

Each screams at you, move faster time runs,

But it moves at the same pace,

No quicker no slower than before,

No different today than it will be tomorrow,

Stand still I challenge you,

Two minutes of your precious manmade time,

Listen, look and think, hear, see, and act,

If each of us makes one kind gesture once a day,

Then the world will smile.

WISH

What would you wish?

What would it be?

A Rock Star maybe?

That I am you and you are me?

Taller perhaps, or a slimmer waist?

Be a runner, win a race?

Now stand by the mirror and take a good look,

It is not the cover but what's in the book.

TODAY

Today

 I am sad,

A little for the world,

And a lot for me,

Why I cannot say,

The morning is bright,

I am healthy, so why?

We sit in our own world,

Cocooned, unappreciative,

We think but not in the right direction,

We feel but not with our hearts,

We sympathise with ourselves, when we should be

grateful,

Today I am sad.

SAD WORDS

Have you ever thought or said?

"What if", "if only",

The saddest words in any language,

If only I had not done that?

What if I had done that?

Stop! Consider!

History can be learned from but never changed,

There is no way back,

So, before they leave your lips, think, learn,

Not what if... but I will not do that again!

Not if only... but I did!

GLASS

A glass of whiskey, a glass of wine,

When going down it feels divine,

When I awake though... not so good!

My head feels like a lump of wood!

I lurch to kettle, make some tea,

That will help... I cannot see!

I sip the tea... ahh... back it comes,

To the bathroom I must run!

I'll never do this thing again,

I pray to God to ease my pain,

By lunchtime though I'm feeling fine,

A glass of whiskey, a glass of wine?

FRIEND

My friend a precious thing,

For friendship must grow and be earned,

It is not when someone gives to you,

That is not friendship,

It is when you give to them,

A contradiction? Perhaps, but not quite,

Friendship is being there, even if you are not,

It is listening, even if the words are hard,

It is not judgmental,

It is honesty, it is truth,

It is forgiveness,

It is the passing of knowledge,

It is friendship,

It is free.

LIGHTNING

The wind howled forcing the rain through the stitching of Steve's jacket making him wonder why he even bothered to wear it. Every few seconds the lightning illuminated the sky. Trudging across the yard moving as quickly as he could against the fierce wind and stinging rain that battered against him. Just a hundred yards but tonight it seemed like miles. Reaching the stable he quickly opened the door but moved more slowly now as he slid inside. He spoke gently as he walked towards the sweating mare, her sides heaving her eyes anxious.

"Steady girl," his hand reached up and stroked the sleek neck, she leaned into him showing that his touch comforted her. Groaning her knees buckled and she sank to the deep straw that covered the floor. Steve knelt beside her not hiding the concern that showed on his face. Her legs rigid as she rolled onto her side. The pain too great her moans pitiful. Her sides heaved her breath ragged. The storm raging outside making it worse. That was five years ago!

Tonight, there was no storm, tonight the weather was beautiful, the sky full of stars no cloud in sight, moths crashed into the outside light, dancing their fluttering ballet as they tried to reach the source of their fascination. Tonight, there was no anxious look in her eyes, tonight she knew. "Well Lightning." Steve said as he stroked the sleek head of the stallion in the adjoining box, looks like you have a sister!

SOMETHING COMPLETELY WEIRD!

$\mathcal{I}$sn't it strange that I sit here? Dreaming of what might be and yet will never be. I wrote a poem in my last book that you will have to find! It tells of a moment that moved me, a moment in which I thought I had found that which had escaped me. I look around and can see for others but not myself. I see their mistakes yet cannot see my own, see their stupidity but cannot see my own. Is this short piece poetry? Is it just the ramblings of a fool? I will leave you to decide if there is any sensibility that you can apply to yourself. For as good as we may try to be we fail, as clever as we may try to be we still fall to foolishness. I am an omnivore and yet love my fellow species... is that hypocrisy... no in truth it is nature, make no mistake she is Queen. A lion can no more eat a Brussel Sprout than fly and yet will protect its pride with its own life. We call it ferocious, wild, a beast, yet we kill it for sport? Something Weird to think about? Today I told a young lady she was beautiful... not because I wanted something but because she was, she thanked me and smiled... beautiful! We fall in love with dreams, it is what we do, we despise, it is what we do. I cannot hate for that is too strong an emotion, too destructive, too parasitic. I love and that in truth is almost as parasitic, for it does eat at you but it is something that can be tempered if you treat it well. The warmth can be held and the cold cast into the abyss... well almost, there is always a little that stays with you. Am I honest? I hope so but then honesty is a matter of opinion. I can be honest in these words and yet still hide the truth... something else weird to think about. I may write from my heart and yet not with an open heart. I voice an opinion that may not be palatable but it is what I feel, if I do, can you appreciate my honesty or will you shun me for the truth? Poetry comes both from the heart, the soul and the imagination for it is feeling, emotion, and possibility. Yet we sometimes fool ourselves as to what is possible and what is reality. If we are honest, do we not all hear what we want to hear and ignore that we do not wish to admit? A piece of advice to all that read it (from a fool) what you have should be cherished, what you wish must stay in the imagination perhaps until others realise that to make change not only do you have to take the first step in that direction but you must also face the truth. It isn't always pleasant, often difficult but once done then the door is open. Now that really is Something Completely Weird.

I have placed this poem in this book as I so like it myself. The sentiment is wonderful but it must be considered that without "The man that doesn't fit in" new horizons would never be seen, new discoveries and so perhaps the man that doesn't fit in is a far greater achiever than realised... perhaps he is the true winner?

There's a race of men that don't fit in,
A race that can't stay still;
So they break the hearts of kith and kin,
And they roam the world at will.
They range the field and they rove the flood,
And they climb the mountain's crest;
Theirs is the curse of the gypsy blood,
And they don't know how to rest.

If they just went straight they might go far;
They are strong and brave and true;
But they're always tired of the things that are,
And they want the strange and new.
They say: "Could I find my proper groove,
What a deep mark I would make!"
So they chop and change, and each fresh move
Is only a fresh mistake.

And each forgets, as he strips and runs
With a brilliant, fitful pace,
It's the steady, quiet, plodding ones
Who win in the lifelong race.
And each forgets that his youth has fled,
Forgets that his prime is past,
Till he stands one day, with a hope that's dead,
In the glare of the truth at last.

He has failed, he has failed; he has missed his chance;
He has just done things by half.

Life's been a jolly good joke on him,
And now is the time to laugh.
Ha, ha! He is one of the Legion Lost;
He was never meant to win;
He's a rolling stone, and it's bred in the bone;
He's a man who won't fit in.

Robert William Service

Something Completely Weird
poems, proverbs, and stuff

Chris Dyer
www.chrisdyerauthor.com

About the Author

Although I have always enjoyed writing my love for horses has been instrumental in most of my books, and my knowledge, which I class myself fortunate to have gathered, as it has helped me in my writing. It has also given me the opportunity to formulate natural remedies for horses. I have an association with an international equine products company. Who are very demanding in their requirements, of which I am glad, and I have produced several formulas that I hope they will market once trials are completed. I would say to all that I feel blessed as I am doing the things that I love to do. It is hard work and I have to say it hasn't always been like this… like everyone, there have been serious low points in my life, even to the point of living on a beach wondering where my next meal would come from. I hope as you read this you will have determination and "never say die". Whatever you are doing or wish to do keep at it, there is a strong possibility that if you are determined enough it will come through for you in the end.

www.ingramcontent.com/pod-product-compliance
Lightning Source LLC
Chambersburg PA
CBHW071433040426
42445CB00012BA/1356